Confessions of a Cyclist

Leanne Bridgewater

NEWTON-LE-WILLOWS

Published in the United Kingdom in 2016
by The Knives Forks And Spoons Press,
122 Birley Street,
Newton-le-Willows,
Merseyside,
WA12 9UN.

ISBN 978-1-909443-74-7

Copyright © Leanne Bridgewater, 2016.

The right of Leanne Bridgewater to be identified as the author of this work has been asserted by her in accordance with the Copyrights, Designs and Patents Act of 1988. All rights reserved. No part of this publication may be reproduced, stored in a retrieval system, transmitted in any form or by any means, electronic, photocopying, recording or otherwise, without prior permission of the publisher.

Confessions of a Cyclist

Winter is coming
When I see the old man with the beard
I know

One ball beside my bedside
One jack-off-lantern on mildew
Round mulberry bush
And *down* dog
Your hound is a throne

One traffic cone wake an ear-woof
As time capsule, a pack of weed
In the hedgerow, the hedgegrow
Image of a gnome grown
Pushing a barrow

I walk tremendously in the tracks of the bracken
And *bramble*, me ambit to be excused
But find myself foraging for magic mushroom

What am I to expect? A pigeon in a plug socket
Bandwidth of open error
A cotton feel for a seal bud
A timer wilt and walken past

My earlobes are marshmallows

Past a Chinese takeaway
The door bells: "nah-nah"
I: "nah-nah, nah-nah-nah"

Once the man: would-you-like-a-fork
Childlike I: condom-i-ments
Mo- mance
Half an ounce of
Eins wright
Field, brother
PLANE

Fly over.

Four tortoises in a fire

Pas ENGER; anger

wheat; germolina
in the linen

A Grin

What becomes of the slum-surrounding
sound of muzzled-out dog-mouth
full of foam?

Open you - and - you **explode**

IRON MAN DAVE IS CRAZY

He wears his hair like a whale

One woman: I'll get the trashcan

A pizza slice and tape splice get along alright.

"When dead dead
will lose my head head

My arms my arms
My knees my knees

Eat takeaway off my knees, please"

What's taken
to the dog-scent
A little irrelevance
elevated, smiling
singing Happy Mondays

some Mondays I wonder about the wasters in the park
always slumped in the same position...

To them:

"I could tell you all kinds of lies.... on the bed... on the ground... planking... on a table..."

Ill gentlemen
walk into scam

*Petite boys at the bus stop crowdfund his ass
and tell him to give over his prescription*

Age pension dis en rage an en counter-balance, unpaid.

Group goes on to shop-raid Aldi, Lidl, Al-Qaeda, Tesco

Mam does marigold, arms folded. I'm tolded
To hang out by an arcade, man comes:
Do you want serenade by a sever run?
To bridge unfold: the water began
Unbolden the bald man
With a soft spot for jack-robins
In jackdaws and lampshades out
On the street, a sofa
Sit on, talk about Neil Armstrong

It's getting late. *Time to talk of jack of late?*

I sit at a station waiting for the dull to pas en glacier

Wheels aspire to the wash-spundicates of some futile

Oil rigged Clothes

knew of better cleanliness

Owned by a someone a little less psycho

Vitamins will fix you

Jay-walking talk.
Bulb young soldiered flowers.
Spew your last words.
Too took and behind you
You're getting picked by the
Ones who are known to pick their nose
Warm before the cold
Before making cake, so you say, clay
don't want on
but can't get off – this love is lost
Teenage tempera rumptun of Trumpton Town delay
On the Hearsall Common, some commoner:

"Get the fluck out of town/way"

Picking out the flowers to put on his mother's grave.

He tells the world: these are on my mum. Not me

Grey haired lady or squirrel. What do I know?

A

sunflower in the window of a red brick house

If you make it larger
The sun will come out

Woman on satellite
Saturday she always waits
On the same bench
In the same coat
The colour of beetroot

As if she's on a beach
She smiles
Admiring some artificial sun
Probably coming from the salon
Opposite the convenience store she sits outside

A man in turban, obviously a bit crazy
On the bench at the end of the arcade
Pigeons surround him
His turban is blue
Maybe the birds think it's a portable part of the sky

The man in turban to the pigeon:

"I could give you all kinds of fries but not to the brain."

At traffic lit
Two women skit a sci-fight
Star wars with an e = stare wars
Lighsabre cat eyes, diamond kites

Wind blows them off
As the lit gets green
They're nowhere to be seen
Apart from in a bus stop
Holding hands. Making love with
The once red envy eyes,
One must've replied.

One ladle idly cry
A lolly looter lullaby
By the beecham cough did they
Upon a counter they portray
In the exotic shop
A reptile dysfunction
Through the window
Two young lads working there
Look like they have nothing else
Going on in their life.
Ought to get a new hobby,
I shout in my head.

You don't know its face

When it's out of its face

Inter inter inter inter

Two fat ladies
Bingo wings
Chatting

Two scrunched up tongues
4 black lungs

Grey deadbeat bird
Dance, macabre

Molecular Prozac
Haven't they learnt about?

Going nowhere

A
 hUmberella

        one that when the rain lands upon

        its inside-out frame, hums

        for the noise of the rain

        comes (flame n co) host, hostile, hot

A fan in funnel with the water scheme

In a bout
Pushing bout
In a boot
Lager lout
In a head
Out a head
Pushing ten-pin
Bowling beat
Jackdaw alley

From pipe lame
Drain pipe-
Tight trousers:
Two men in.

WOMEN

As we cycle

there's one of us in front

in lycra

One peach derriere on two sticks
Like a double toffee-apple

Cheer a dog on and dog will take to the
pelvis like a cyclist into a bus

SNIFFS

... white boy **ELVIS**

thrust

From hell - eco - bacta in exterior

my deer is an antler

glub trotter,

Barry White shite on a car radio in Wiltshire

Rubber tyres speed

A buttered skid from autumn wet leafoilage
Age of the third child of the mother: season.
Red as demon in denim matching suit
Tie are the cut boots, the styled hair
All the laugh is
In a minute dead will buckle its shoe

Blue

Black Rabbits

"These boys don't know their arse from their elbow"

A cyclist run over on the A road

The body clock

pounding on the pavement

broken bones

lorries

                                        loads of passengers from the bus

                                              that's just pulled over

Lozenges

Slippers

Fly over

Bus driver:

"I could give you all kinds of fries but not to the brain."

Light goes when winter comes

ICEBERG CALIBRE

In dark, the street lights hum

Penetration is...

Lactic acid.

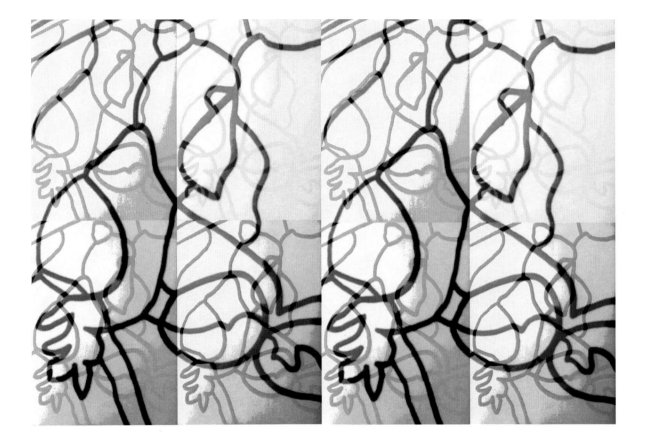

The fan is in humming mode.

A humming bird has lost its worth

SOLDIERED to the air-conditioning

set on an off-white wall

Stomach lining
In it
A
Fish
Tipped upside down
A bowl
Out of:
The sky is the water
The water is the sky

FILTER

A man hacking off a fence :

Lumber JACK

daw alley, where's
 the Allen   key?

Brake heavens with E's –
up all night with spud eyes,
busting formulas, hopping joints
questioning, e's a she's a
FOREIGNER

FANtasy

Reigns, deer – too many low key Don Quixote's.
Exotic, fans, mandala – trance?

A fan will dance when no one is looking

Squint eyes into the sun and open
the arms as wide as the weekend eyes

Windmills are only alive when they dance

What have I become?

see a vortext

a passenger; read me the circumference. Share me thoughts

talk at me : con ference and adherence

"Pear. A conference pear"

The fan is loud and takes over **our** meeting

Ambience is conditional: air

Doodles in my employment
pants the adhoc answer to
"what do we do"

"I agree", it's a policy decision.

A bike the size of a hybrid entangles jargon in rhythm

We trapped the world in a jar.

Push the sky over

watch the stars fall out

You know you are a bowling ball

Rolling down the hill into the back of a van
I meet a man who is a toad:

I stood before a toad
I asked it 'how'd it goed'
it said it know'd not to go on
but said in flux, like saffron,
rich and pointless,
all over the place,
all way back to ones abode

The jack lumbers you with a hammer

You know we've knocked your lights out
Stan-d
Only on your right leg
We'll fight your arm off
Don't tell us when to cross

- Pedestry harder, you willow

A
tree on
a
chopper bike

Elm street,
muppet tops

[STAMMER]

Toad says, "you have been jumped, wise man"

Lady poshes pram up hill
In the act she never bends her legs
How can a short person still look short in heels?

Wurthering / worrying

Heights

&
tacky eyelashes placed over car lights:

"You will feel no shame"

A remote-control drone hovers over Walsgrave parade

And here again we wade in traffic

Calm the carpet
Knees deep in
Broad arm bean stalking face walking
We'll die here
Names engraved

In road rage
Raven on edge
Bite a meal open-skin
Ring a rosen ride rosette
On the internet, biker you met

Til e text, tilt

A lane to the left

Science cannot fully explain how a bicycle stays upright

Cycling against the wind
is performing arts to Nicky Morgan

NICKY MORE GAN GUN,   IS GANG GREEN

NICKY MORE GAN GUN,   IS GANG GREEN

NICKY MORE GAN GUN,   IS GANG GREEN

NICKY MORE GAN GUN,   IS

MORE GREEN THAN EVER GREEN

SHE'S ON THE RUN

NICKY MORE GAN GUN

NICKY MORE GAN GUN

Put me up your old jack slack
And I will be your heroin
Put me up on your rucksack back
And I will take your old bike back
Put up will be shutting up
My bike can hold the shopping
While you can hold the baby
The voice of the background music is a humming
Bird of the rusty chain
Side-saddled riddled worm

Upright piano, you know how you do...

Pio Near

A Piano And   a Pan

A pioneer of a pie in a pan cooking by a piano, conducting wave fragments. Heat: micro. Heart (attack). A cord of an apple to... fine grrrrs...grip...

rest the pedal in the gutter, on to the kerb
where an old kebab moulds

Wheels go over a furby
Of a cat or fat rat
In fathom and anthem
You can't shake your head to
The man who jogs then paves cement with phlegm

Every cycle is a mission. Play games with passers-by,
smiling at every person you encounter

The Practice of Happiness lies within
the inverted bridge-shape before your chin

There's some place I pass called Wyken
I hardly encounter it as a person,
more as a passive thought
of place between A and B

In the alley towards the train station

two dogs fighting:

"paws for fought"

Before a train comes

Smells of oil-rum vacuum habitat a rabbit pie of dust bun
It's where you run from
Over a train line

2 rabbits -
They don't look wild

They've escaped from a hatch

In a garden
Once domesticated

Finally, these guys have a run of their lives

I ask the train station if she has any knowledge of them

"no, not seen them before...
will you call the rspca?"

bobbling around
probably enjoying
their time of freedom

I conversate with the inner meat:

'long-life of living in a little wooden box
or
a shorter one in the wild with freedom'

I smile on behalf of them and let the silence do the rescuing

A Compromise
without a handshake
comes to mind
a kilo maker in the half-lit baker-y.
Find the light on, and the bread oven fan
and keys to each 'bread-winner'
in an open plan glove box, hot-desking office

Opera playing from a stereo
of a man shaking fists, and
"First is first…"

4 miles lost had got me to
turn to a cyclist
for directions

He reckoned he could 'take me there'
And so I followed,
And as we took off,
I barely moved and he was nearly out of shot

He slew the slaw down.
This person is a pensioner, I thought.

Now and again my hen, it's a NEW GENERATION

Now and again my hen, it's a NEW GENERATION
Now and again my hen, it's a NEW GENERATION
Now and again my hen, it's a NEW GENERATION
Now and again my hen, it's a NEW GENERATION
Now and again my hen, it's a NEW GENERATION
Now and again my hen, it's a NEW GENERATION
Now and again my hen, it's a NEW GENERATION
Now and again my hen, it's a NEW GENERATION
Now and again my hen, it's a NEW GENERATION

Raconteur racoon-rat
under poison swan,
bury all until we are one

El der ly
flow eryl
Non floral
Non choral
Exc. Songs of praise
One day
We may beat you at chess
The next
Outside a chippie
A senior
Beats the brew from your collar bone
As your shirt scuffs
Dirty collars
Kissed

The gran came with garnishing
As she catches you in the
Eyes you watch from
Through the binoculars
Collars
Are Tory-incorporated

Navy skydives a police siren
Turns your back on
And you have to ask
How old is she, really
And is she taken
By the gremlins
Who fist-punched my
Last dear was a porsche,

*Some old hippy lay on a bench
in pretence to be asleep*

*It was outside Prêt Monge
He looked pretty monged out
- wasn't their coffee -
This granny
came and sat on top of him
after taking a pee in Gosford park
as I cycled past her with my friend
we said 'good on her'
and I would have thought
the passers-by would be all technical
grammatically perfecting the
angle for their Instagram account
I was wrong. They don't want to see it all*

I didn't even have to look at her.
She was smiling anyway.

They thought she was an incubator

Master

Master

    BATOR

Mac arthur's back on prozac
he couldn't find his mind
outside was dark and empty

so he went to undress the switch of his lamplight
but it didn't operate the outside lamplight

I cut the boy splinter in the standard newsletter
a staple to stick the pageants together
their make-up run to make out with the weather
we run the light with laughter
electricity with ecstasy
put a crazy lipstick
smoother yourself
here's to wrecking with
neglect of the sexuality impersonate

Fuck you sonnet.

Went for an issue with a keyhole
weren't you the Tudor pole
of the totem smile?

Caught distrunk

aback a rizla cheque off with your hand

you go smoking in the capital

the capital of Apple

I ctrl and command an ass that offers with a donkey proverb

I inch dirt a rocky path to your grandma's house
we throw rocks at the window

the cat meows

Sunflower's cried   "It's time...

we go back to a mountain
lit torch
teach Latin in the literature,
Boy George, look at ya
chaining people to radiators
stashing cookies in your jar
amounts of white stuff go for washing tablets
as your lips crumple them together"

It's not time to put clothes out. It's dark outside

"I called my dad"

"Chocolate makes you wide...and is this where rabbits hide?.."

[Answer to await]

Care to talk of Jack of late?

Spare associate
tends to clean up where they left off
to the top right some plane
takes off its wings
frees itself from the sky
what once
was an alibi

In Baghdad bombs fly

He said he'd rather be choc-o-block than choc-o-late

Shoulder-pads give strain

many veins are strings, wrung out on a cello
they tend to kiss but share a creep in the door

hours after a face funnels - through - some whisper - through -
the saline smells - and chemist air, - she turns to me

" heavens you easily, pleased"

Questions happen to ask around the circle

- they think they're purple

Mumps

podium shade

calibre

5 watt bulb

Because

no one cares to see

seaside | incisions

Do me pretty, legion. Social club stares

PIGEONS

A snooker club hosts still-uppers from the night before, ask
"what you after" they holler
On the way to work – 7am.

A cycling holiday

Cycling behind a hearse makes you stop and think hard...

About the time it has taken you to get from there to <u>here</u>

Lord beat interfere, atmosphere heaver in phlegm.

Make a world out of them...

You left your sad-earned horse
a dog the colour of a gherkin

One alpha male snook off to court a mannequin
Keep it coming, her plastic face said.

She froze him, right there in the snow

A shop window with
**"nothing to see here
makes the lips go…"**

Exclamation marks are tarts.
They want all of the attention.

The windows clam.

Steamy kitchen offers potatoes boiling in a pan

Pansexuality is an attraction towards any gender

exPANsion.
    A pan enlarges by the soaking up of the boiling water inside it

all around pans
and pots
and pitches
of sound
glorious sound
in such instance:
a micro

wave
                                            a see

a   coyote

CAVE

an ass for an ape, a 4 tune > 4 chimes. What for?
Chi of M.E man's got. Down with symptom. Chick-pock?

RAVE

Are you really interested in shapes?

What is a vertical ego?

*Gradient smiles go radiant in suns,
on one de-rain-gy day*

A wiiji board - wii games now playing with the dead. Priced at £259.99

or a shameful oulipoja mojito

            e e only e eeee's well bladdered

So my dad turned into some kind of fruit…

…papaya

News beat Armstrong
Nuclear deterrent
Errands.

and my mother, called ma, I call her, she went too

a ma-n-derine

but you see
                        the man always butts in

A shop in the City Arcade offers Mehndi for the scalp

Before home, from Spongate to Butts Lane, over a misshapened wall, deliver the Sherbourne river:

"The water sustains me without even trying"

Chuck the bag on to the living room floor

In it
A

dead shirt,
screwed up and folded round a lunch box paradox

"I'll eat you someday"

THE SHIRT

"I started working on the protocollar off the cuff. I kept the project on my sleeve but kept the pen where I wrote it out in the chest pocket over my left breast."

THE SHIRTY

"I wore my red on the sleeve. It slipped. Menstrual minstrel people came adancing, applauding, annoying the fluster out of."

THE SKIRTING BOARD as a table, with copper, could be copper, could just be... dirt

We chat of thee over a shared coffee in a cafe
where the flies bathe on top of sweet-favourites

French cafe
casual writer style
boring poetry
possibly cabaret

note instead
the waitress blending vegetables
the noise
is noise
is nice

One asks for advice,

how much of an angle does your leg bend when pedalling?

A magpie winks me to look at a hedgehog
lining the kerb of the road

I get off my bike and inspect

A cop car passes and feels obliged to nosey, vocal:

"He's ok. Just corpse. I'd rather him dead than   you."

They drive hearse pace

- I wait until they pass to move the hog to a better place.

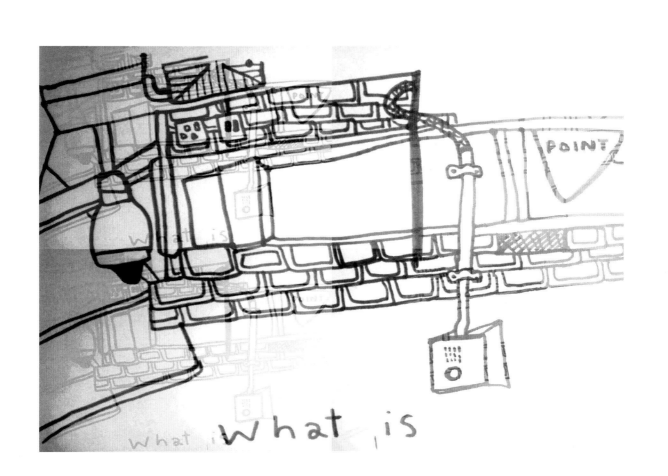

A spoof in the schwartznega suit and leather seats

Their cassette like the Wiltshire get -
"It's the sound of da police" (KRS-ONE)

un momento plea

Pace | place | maker

a swan on one bloat of a gun in iguana
like cat- man-do and mehndi

it's why we tend to take our own path
(a cat happens to task a ravel in the rizla)

Like rather sit in the park and crack open the weed pot
rosemary in bush
thorn for the phone job

Don't go work
don't go the pool where you'll drown
sit round the soil
gents of earthly boil
lay on the grass for a while
would rather list up the piss of a squirrel
to be in the real world
ain't nothing real

Smoke the load
heavy leaves
lighter eyes
roll around
in the lies of the lawns in the cracks of the dawns

Crack open the weed pots
thinks lots less
haven't bothered to guess
shattered like the past
as if these moments always last

I pitched the head a past a stage
rather sit by the haze
watch out flow-s
the thorns!

Heavy glow
hibiscus bliss
hadn't bothered to guess
it's these things
like mistaking sweet apple juice for piss

A human in capable:
... but toad, not banana,
please, saffron!

A heavy gun.

BANG

*I thought it was not my place to know
where toad grow from and go back to
but since toad told me I asked what room
was one normally situated in*

A.. a... a.... mush room, he jokes/croaks

Knees bespoked,

I asked the man who borrowed playsets from the library, could he ever forget what happened at the bus stop?

His hands shook away from his head as his toes curled

He sees his father's face in his mother's face

Compromise?

Hip youngsters wearing body warmers with altered persona

Two doors down a neck of the

                                          A
                              Wooden boat
                                  Afloat
                        On the motorway
                                HUM
                              Sledging
                                  In it
A slum on the elderflower brew
                                  Slow
Talking over repeating swigs

                    We talk about these twigs that build houses

                                      and plans to build on greenland x 10

                        a gruffalo

Heavy hens will cream a goat

                    a dandelion
                          a
                        lion
                    a flat tyre
                    a hyphen
                a bike, on one
                    bickering

TYERSOME LULLERING:

A mother tells her 3 year old boy to lose a moral

Boy soma special place
One day wanting to be
A
Brick
Layer

In material, a park in the halfway home.

Some are into cabaret.

One red-road faces delays through a body on the floor

POT
HOLES
GALORE

"Limer licks your lips as you say stag-hunting is your main hobby"

I cycle by your house and smash your window.

- "Willow tree, y'know"

Rabbit holes glow in the night

Daggered heart bumbaclart nicks my bike saddle and nothing else.

Closer to the house

See

Jack

Run

Jack

"I live at the one with the lights on"

DAW-n through curtains of lazy eyelids

Cycling means to alter the backpack straps

[A budgie happens to crack]

Smart ass rubbed against his glass

for a window cleaner puts his elbows into it.

[Friday night's Meal Wear-M]

CRETINS

Things look tinier from far away

I took his pathway to decay
A tinter grey on macabre

Love in a shoebox flat

Dad asks, how many giraffes can fit in a Mini?

Mother of the hardship
Extraordinary tinker
Earth, that is.

Around it, season
see son, you know
you are a bowling ball
in the black pool table
one's fable is another's
bandwagon

Before I wrap up,
I see the bearded man
on my way from the library
on Tuesday's and Friday's

He stops and turns to me
and shouts

"This is the last time I talk of jack of late"

Jackdaw went stray. Elderman in clay
sculpted for another world
sun billed
A family of four
go out cycling one day
down the parade

I felt a dragon as I breathed into the balaclava

Calibre?

until the drunk man can hardly withstand

he puffed the clouds from the sky into his eyes
with fables, viagra, juniper oil and through soiling the sun
on his travels towards the big Asda

Whatever will we become?

over a church,
some envelope of light performs a sabre and reveals itself

because it's summer now and

BEARDS

They never fail to amaze me

Drunk kids displaying unconditional feelings
over cans of Stella

Jog on

In sun, there's no need to leave the light on.
One bulben mackerel flower
mocks a duck and picking up
the washing drying out on the floor.

Spin all y'like,
wheels on a bike.

DANSE BEAT MAC ABRE

rusty chain adjust and comes astop

I offered the bearded man the sunflower. He told me it's still in the ground, so how could it even be an offer. I said, ok, not an offer, but an offering, to know, that something, is *growing*

A lady in the bus stop shouts out, "got a light"

I say neigh, but the sky has

[only a crack]

Sun comes
when the beard goes
and bees kneed into skin
a little sun to begin with
open toe shoes
in the beginning
give conditioning
and air, light air-conditioning

*Head Phone booths weed roots of
auburn ray-gun hair of one
summer songs in the sun*

We once both lost the woman of the sun but now she is with us again

Light comes to grow the stem

Home again, stamen

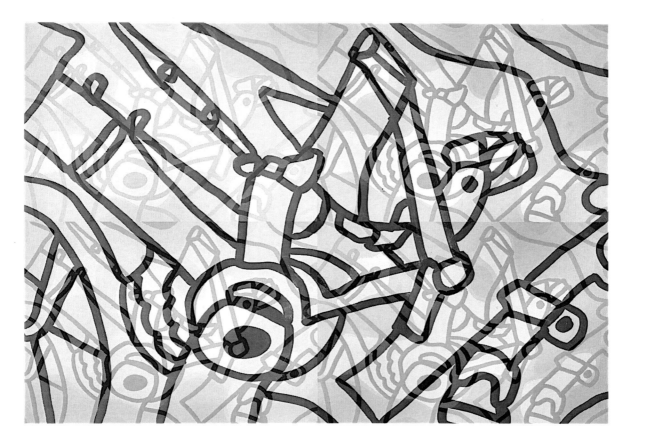